PEST

Photography
PÁL HUBER

Text
TIBOR IZSÁK

Translation
GÉZA KERÉNYI

CONTENTS

THE CASTLE DISTRICT

In ancient times the Celts recognized how important the location of Budapest was. Much later, and after many a stormy episode, Béla IV, the 13th century Hungarian king, realized the importance of the Castle Hill. The hill stretches for 1,500 m along the right bank of the Danube and rises to a height of between 60 and 70m. A surviving record tells us that Béla IV declared that a fortress was to be built here in 1255.

The fortress has an irregular layout around a keep. It was erected upon the rim of the limestone rock of the Southern foothills. The tuff cavities, which extend over the whole area of the Castle Hill, include caves and have been tunneled into over the ages. The core of the fortified area was the Stephen Tower and its attached living quarters. At its north-west corner, there was housing separated by a crenelated wall with turrets. The Kelenföld Gate stood at the Southern edge of the hill, beneath the Great Round Bastion of later times. As the Castle was built and enlarged, the defense zone and the outer wall, with closed yards between them, also grew larger.

After centuries of destruction and reconstruction, excavation (still going on) now allows us to see what the 15th-16th century bulwarks looked like. From the South, they extended in a wedge with the now renovated Mace Tower (early 15th century) and the entrance tower of the Round Bastion. The Castle and the area it protected soon became densely populated and took a leading role in the life of the country.

The golden age of the whole Castle District came during the reign of King Matthias (1458-1490). The Royal Palace and buildings around it reflected the glory of that great Renaissance King. Even now a glimpse into a courtyard of one of the surviving houses allows you to experience the historic atmosphere of the whole quarter.

For centuries this was the heart of the nation, with most of the offices of state located here.

The Second World War brought tremendous devastation here, too. No more than four of the 170 or so buildings on Castle Hill survived. It was not until ten years after the war that the work of restoration got underway here. Fortunately, the old style was retained when the houses, streets and buildings were restored. Today's visitor can enjoy the old beauty of the Castle District and see how it has managed to mirror the country's history in its stones.

The Buda Castle District was declared part of the World Heritage by UNESCO in 1988.

The Matthias Church and the Fishermen's Bastion. Coming up along Hunyadi János út from Clark Ádám tér, a turn to the left in the road provides a sight of the harmony of the Matthias Church and the Fishermen's Bastion. Your eye is immediately caught by the colored tiles (produced by the world-

famous Zsolnay manufacture in Pécs) that cover the roof of the church.

Here stands the Kolozsvári brothers' statue of St. George on the right. On the other side is the bronze statue of János Hunyadi, the great general who recaptured Belgrade from the Turks, a victory that has been celebrated all over the Christian world by the tolling of the noon Angelus bell ever since 1456.

The Jesuit Stairs lead up through the Fishermen's Bastion to the Matthias Church. The edges of the stairs and walkways are decorated by neo-Romanesque ornamentation.

3

The view of Buda Castle from the Citadel. A breathtaking view of Buda Castle can be had from the Citadel on top of Gellért Hill. The architectural history of the Castle goes back to the 13th century. The royal residence was developed over the three hundred years between the Mongol invasion (1241) and the Turkish occupation (1541). The fortifications and palace, frequently ravaged, burned and looted in the wars that plagued the country were rebuilt again and again. The reconstruction completed by 1412 was commissioned by King Sigismund - who was also the Holy Roman Emperor. The second half of the 15th century saw the golden age of

The Chapel of the Palace had once stood alone in the Northern part of the Castle. The Gothic chapel, later merging into the Palace, was first mentioned in 1360. A twin-level and buttressed castle-chapel, its three rose windows overlook the yard. Part of it has been fully restored, using the abundance of fragments that were uncovered during excavation work.

King Matthias' Well. The highlight of the large space in the middle of the Buda Castle is Alajos Stróbl's statue (1904) known as the Matthias Well. The king, represented as a huntsman, is accompanied by the legendary Beautiful Ilonka and a falconer.

Buda Castle, under the reign of King Matthias when it was the center of administration, diplomacy, the arts and sciences. (King Matthias' sumptuous library was also located here.) The palace's present appearance is due to the neo-Baroque reconstruction that the architects Miklós Ybl and Alajos Hauszmann were responsible for.

The Buda Cable Car. This two-track car takes you up 100 m from the Buda end of the Chain Bridge to Szent György tér in the Castle District. Inspired by Count Ödön Széchenyi, it was inaugurated on May 2, 1870. The carriages were originally driven by a steam engine. Stone ramparts flank both sides of the line and are connected by bridges, so it is possible to make the steep climb on foot above the cable car's track.

The track, like all of the Castle District, was destroyed in World War II. With great popular acclaim, it went back into operation again in 1986.

The Great Arms of Hungary. If you take the Cable Car up from Clark Ádám tér, you cannot help but notice a huge version of the Great Arms of Hungary patterned into the wall beside the station. This was originally placed here in 1880 and has once again been restored to its pristine glory. The national arms in the middle are surrounded by the arms of the provinces that once belonged to Hungary.

The Palace of Buda. The roof line of the Palace, some 300 m long and parallel with the Danube, is perhaps most spectacular from here, Clark Ádám tér. The hilltop is dominated by this Hauszmann designed wing.

At the southern end of the building, slightly lower in height, is the Baroque Maria Theresa wing.
After the post-war restoration, the Palace houses, within the National Gallery, a permanent exhibition of important 19th and 20th century Hungarian painting and sculpture. It is also the venue for exhibitions of both Hungarian and foreign art. The National Széchenyi Library is located in the West wing of the Palace. It is available to all interested visitors.

The Matthias Church and the Holy Trinity Column. The most important and the most cherished church in Budapest is the Matthias Church on Szentháromság tér. A church has stood on this site ever since the beginning of the 13th century. Like many other of Europe's celebrated churches, it has been rebuilt several times. Thus, the two lateral naves were vaulted up to match the height of the center in the 14th century. During the Turkish occupation, the church was the High Mosque. After the ousting of the Turks, it was rebuilt in a Baroque form.

Its current shape dates from the 19th century, when it was reconstructed under Frigyes Schulek's guidance. The Gothic spire of the more than 700 year old church is one of the features of the cityscape.

Szentháromság tér itself was named after the Holy Trinity Column that stands in its center.

The Matthias Church. The church is emotionally overwhelming: Gothic arches and splendid columns. The church has three naves, is of the basilica type laid out in the French pattern. The Southern spire, completed in 1470, displays in stone the coat of arms of the Hunyadis, King Matthias' family.Because of its splendid acoustics, the church has long been an important venue for concerts.
Ferenc Liszt's Coronation Mass was premiered here in 1867, so too was Zoltán Kodály's Buda Castle Te Deum in 1936.
The present interior of the church is Frigyes Schulek's work. There is a museum in the crypt and the oratory which contains works of religious art.

Stained glass windows of the Matthias Church.
The church received new, high windows in the mid-14th century. The present three large stained glass windows represent the Virgin Mary, St. Margaret and St. Elisabeth, while the round window depicts Christ as the Lamb of God. The paintings and the glass are by Bertalan Székely and Károly Lotz.

The Fishermen's Bastion. This section of the rampart of the old wall faces Pest. It is located above the fishermen's village of olden times and a fish market was still being regularly held beside the church in the 1830s - hence the name of the bastion.

After defeating the Hungarians in the 1848/49 War of Independence, the Government of Vienna had all the bastions on Castle Hill pulled down. These present terraced promenades were built on their old foundations in the 1900s and were designed by Frigyes Schulek. With its five neo-Romanesque roofed towers and a sixth, multi-level main tower, all in white limestone, the Fishermen's Bastion is a fine vantage point. The stairways on both sides are adorned with the statues of Álmos and Előd, two of the leaders of the Magyar tribes that conquered our homeland. Sculptures are also found in the covered part of the

The Fishermen's Bastion with St. Stephen's Statue. Near the Matthias Church, the arcades of the Fishermen's Bastion are a spectacular background for the large equestrian bronze statue of St. Stephen, which stands on the site of the old fish market. It was created by Alajos Stróbl, the pedestal reliefs are the work of Frigyes Schulek.

The Fishermen's Bastion by night. An evening visit here, when it is brightly illuminated, is unforgettable. Again, it is a magnificent vantage point offering indelible impressions of the city at night.

The Northern tower includes a pleasant restaurant, a bar and a wine-shop.

T-shaped stairs of the central axis. Above the corridors, the towers are connected by balconies.

The Fishermen's Bastion, one of the city's most beautiful landmarks, has never been used as defense works. All the Pest cityscape and the Danube Bend are visible from here on a clear day, a sight that draws both locals and visitors.

The Hilton Hotel. Constructing a new hotel over Gothic and Baroque remnants was a complex artistic challenge, demanding the provision of first class hotel services and the preservation of what had survived the past. The result can clearly be seen in the harmonious amalgamation of the spire of the old Church of St. Nicholas into the facade of the building.

The picture shows the statue of Pope Innocent XI erected to commemorate the 250th anniversary of Buda's liberation from the Turks.

A Glimpse into a Courtyard. Let us look into the courtyard of a small Baroque house, which faithfully reflects the medieval atmosphere of the houses in the Castle District. These houses were renovated in the 19th century, but retained old features often combining the then traditional Baroque style with Classical, Gothic or Zopf (Austrian late Baroque) elements (Úri utca 28).

Castle ambi-ance. From the heart of the Castle District, Szentháromság tér, hackney coaches can be hired. They invoke the past and contribute to the atmosphere of the neighbor-hood. A drive in one allows you to comfortably inspect the historic streets and feel their romantic beauty.

Tárnok utca is the most important, and the broadest, street of the Castle District, almost a square by virtue of its width. It is linked with Úri utca by a series of small lanes. It leads right to Szentháromság tér. Clearly visible in the picture is the house at number 14-16 Tárnok utca, which demonstrates the wall painting style of the 16th century.
At present, the street houses a variety of gift shops and restaurants.

A Baroque House. A beautifully reconstructed neo-Baroque building, which was originally erected in the 1720s. Its facade richly ornamented by arms and statues, the house retained its Baroque remnants when it assumed its current form in 1904. Its columned entrance and its height make the building stand out among its neighbors (Úri utca 58).

Bécsi kapu tér. The houses of the Castle District which evoke the atmosphere of olden times are adjoined by the huge block of the National Archives, built by Samu Pecz in the years of World War I (1914-1918). It houses the nation's most important collection of documents, deeds and letters. The building frames the square on the North (Bécsi kapu tér 4).

ALONG THE DANUBE

Budapest contains an almost 30 km stretch of the Danube, flowing North to South between Buda and Pest. Both halves of the municipality face the river. The Danube links Budapest to eight countries by water, turning the Hungarian capital into a seaport, too.

Several of the city's most important and impressive public buildings line the embankments. A visitor may be under the impression that the city developed over thousands of years. In actual fact though, only the core of the settlement, medieval Buda and a few streets in Pest, have been occupied for several centuries. After the disastrous flood in 1838 when Pest was devastated, dikes were constructed on both banks of Central Europe's greatest river. This was also when the two-level flood control system of the quays was put in place. The lower quay is often swamped by high water even today.

The city, of which all Hungarians are justly proud, developed very rapidly. In a few short leaps and bounds, it caught up with other major cities over the last 150 years. Indeed, the image we have of it today had emerged by the turn of the century.

On the Pest bank, the much celebrated Dunakorzó, the riverside promenade, is a favorite giving a spectacular view across the Danube of the Castle, the Gellért Hill and the Buda Hills. This stretch between the Elizabeth Bridge and the Chain Bridge is reserved for pedestrians. Thousands upon thousands stroll or sit around here enjoying the sunshine, especially from spring to autumn.

The Pest riverside was lined by a row of elegant hotels before the war, but these fell victim to the siege in 1944-45. The area has been redeveloped with a number of new buildings, including hotels. The Castle Hill and the Gellért Hill rise on the Buda side of the Danube. Medicinal baths have been built to harness the thermal springs. The view from Pest is superbly framed by the hills of Buda. The unique loveliness of the landscape underlines the situation of the town. The baths by the Danube and a significant number of the spas have survived war damages and continue to operate in their original form.

Houses of Parliament. Construction was begun in 1885. The architect was Imre Steindl, who had visited many countries to study the styles of various epochs. Eclecticism, combining a number of styles, seems to have been the guiding principle in his planning.

The building is 268 m long and covers an area of nearly 18,000 m^2 and was completed by 1906. The layout, the

arrangement and linkage of space are Baroque in nature, but the architecture is neo-Gothic. The exterior is decorated by 88 statues. The main facade overlooks the Danube. This frontage features statues of the seven chieftains who led the Magyar tribes that conquered Hungary, and sculptures of Hungarian kings.

The main entrance, the Lion Gate, opens onto Kossuth Lajos tér. On this side, there are statues of Princes of Transylvania, military commanders and valiant soldiers.

The highest point of the rib vaulted dome, which is supported by 16 clusters of pillars, is 96 m above street level. The gigantic building grouped around ten courtyards, has 27 entrances and 29 staircases. On both sides of the dome are the two assembly halls, one holding 450 and the other 300.

The ornamental staircase of Parliament.

The Kossuth Lajos tér main entrance leads to a wide ornamental staircase, laid out in the Baroque style. The ceiling frescoes, The Apotheosis of Legislation and The Glorification of Hungary, are by Károly Lotz. Imre Steindl's bust by Alajos Stróbl stands in a niche over the landing, while the figure of two pages on each side is supported by brackets along the lateral rows of pillars.

The ornamental staircase leads to the domed hall at the center of the building. The magnificent hall hosts numerous ceremonies. A gigantic Christmas tree is placed here every year.

The assembly chamber of the Parliament.

Left of the domed hall, beyond the lobbies is the U-shaped assembly chamber with the Speaker's rostrum, the sloping rows of seats and the galleries separated by arches with tracery. It is surrounded by corridors on each side.

The picture shows the Assembly Chamber lit by tall Gothic windows. The walls are decorated by frescoes representing the National Assembly of 1848 and the coronation of 1867. Arcades divided into three sections are on the ground level with a triple tier of boxes above.

Parliament by night. The Parliament presents an unforgettable sight when viewed from the Danube by night. Fabulously reflected over the water surface are the rows of windows, the open vaulted galleries and the dome soaring between two high towers.

Margaret Island. In the 13th century, there was already a Dominican convent on the island. King Béla IV's daughter grew up there. Her name was Margaret and she was to be canonized later. The island was named after the Princess.

The medieval settlements disappeared and life on the island only resumed when the Palatine József built a palace here and planted rare trees, ornamental shrubbery and flowers at the end of the 18th century. Particular favorites are the huge plane trees with their lush foliage.

The island is 2,500 m long and 500 m wide. It is rich in thermal waters; the Grand Hotel Margaret Island was built on a strikingly beautiful site to exploit these, and the island also boasts various sports facilities, restaurants and an open air theater.

Batthyány tér. This lovely square catches the eye from the opposite, Pest, side of the Danube. There are many fine Baroque houses on the bank near the Buda foothills. St. Ann's Church, one of Hungary's most valuable Baroque buildings, faces onto the square.

A two-story house standing on the Fö utca side of Batthyány tér is perhaps the noblest example of the Rococo style in Budapest.

View of the Danube and the Chain Bridge. Construction of the Chain Bridge was begun in 1839 upon Count István Széchenyi's initiative; the English engineer T. W. Clark produced the designs. His namesake Adam Clark was in

charge of the work, which took ten years. It was the first permanent bridge connecting the two cities of Buda and Pest. The cables of the 380 m long bridge are suspended over the top of the two triumphal arches and fixed to underground chambers. The stone lions at both ends of the bridge are local favorites. The arches were broadened by 1 m when the bridge was rebuilt following its demolition by German sappers during the Second World War.

The picture, taken from the Buda side, shows the Hungarian Academy of Sciences, the Gresham Palace, the Ministry of the Interior and, behind them, the dome of the Basilica.

Illuminated Chain Bridge. The sight of the Chain Bridge sparkling in a string of lights in its evening glory is captivating. Behind it, the floodlit Buda Castle rises majestically towards the night skyline.

Fireworks display. Every year on August 20, the Feast of Saint Stephen, who founded the Kingdom of Hungary, a truly spectacular fireworks display lights up the embankments of Danube, almost like in daytime.

The Elizabeth Bridge. The Elizabeth Bridge was one of the landmarks in the turn-of-the-century development of the capital. Antal Kherndl's calculations were used by Aurél Czekelius in his design of the bridge, which took six years to build (1897 to 1903). Its span of 290 m was the biggest in the world for a suspension bridge until 1926. The total length of the bridge was 379 m.

That bridge, destroyed during World War II, was rebuilt at the original site by 1964. The new Erzsébet híd is also a suspension bridge and is the main East-West artery of Budapest, crossing the Danube out of the Inner City.

Hotels on the Pest Embankment. Modern hotels have been erected to replace those on the Danube bank destroyed during World War II. Among them are the Atrium Hyatt, the Forum and the Marriott. Between this row of hotels and the Danube, connecting Roosevelt tér with Március 15 tér, stretches the Dunakorzó or Danube Promenade. Near Roosevelt tér, on Eötvös tér, at the northern end of the Dunakorzó stands the statue of the Baron József Eötvös, a leading figure of the Reform Era. At the southern end of the Dunakorzó, Március 15 tér is the site of a statue of the great Hungarian poet Sándor Petőfi, which was unveiled in 1871. The Dunakorzó, closed to motor vehicles, is a favorite of tourists, too.

The Liberty Bridge with the Gellért Hotel. This bridge spans the Danube for 365 m and work on it commenced in 1894. The opening ceremony in 1896 was attended by the Emperor Franz Joseph. The transversal bracing between the pillars has ornamental gates supporting the mythical Turul birds at their top and the great arms of Hungary in the middle. The bridge connects the Small Boulevard encircling the Inner City of Pest with Szent Gellért tér, at the foot of Gellért Hill on the other side of the river.

St. Gellért's Memorial. The monument marks the place where Bishop St. Gellért was martyred, rolled down the hill into the Danube in a barrel in 1046.

The picture shows the Gellért Hotel, which with its medicinal baths was completed by 1918. This de luxe hotel has long been a favorite of visitors to the capital, attracted by its famous restaurant and thermal baths.

The Liberation Monument. Atop the Gellért Hill, 130 m above the Danube, Zsigmond Kisfaludy Stróbl's monument occupies the most eye-catching spot in the city. The bronze female figure together with its pedestal reaches a height of 40 m. The Citadel looms behind.

THE INNER CITY

Today's Inner City has been settled since Roman times and is in fact built over the groundwork of that Roman community. It has always been the site of an important river crossing. The part of the town girded by a city wall originally dates from the 13th century, and Pest only expanded out of that area at the beginning of the 19th century. It occupied the semicircle from the Liberty Bridge to Deák Ferenc utca. Remnants of the old wall can still be seen in a few places, as in Kálvin tér - where its vestiges are marked out. By the end of the 18th century, the still walled town had taken a leading role in the rapidly developing fields of education, cultural life, trade and industry. Fine town houses were built one after another in the Inner City during the 18th and 19th century. Vörösmarty tér, north of Deák Ferenc utca is also an inseparable part of what is traditionally regarded as the Inner City, as is the Dunakorzó, which extends as far as the Chain Bridge.

Today, the inner part of Pest is considered to be the area from the Margaret Bridge to the Liberty Bridge along the left bank of the Danube. It is bordered by the Szent István körút on the north, and the Small Boulevard on the east and south. This is where the overwhelming majority of national institutions are found.

The most illustrious streets of the Inner City, Váci utca and Petőfi Sándor utca, run parallel with the Danube. Here and in the connecting streets between them, as well as in the romantic shopping cellars are Budapest's most elegant shops. Local and foreign banking houses have also done their best to find premises here. The most exquisite confectionery in the city is also to be had here, in the Romantic-Eclectic Gerbeaud building on Vörösmarty tér at the northern end of Váci utca. Of the many restaurants in the center, the 100 éves étterem (The Hundred Years Old) radiating the spirit of olden days, is an interesting historical building. Built in 1756, it is practically the only Baroque house preserved in the original style in Pest.

Klotild Palaces. These twin palaces frame the Pest end of the Elizabeth Bridge and extend as far as Ferenciek tere, named after Koburg Klotild Mária, who had them built. They house up-market shops and prime

offices. There is a casino and the showroom of Budapest Gallery in the building on the southern side of the street. On the northern side of this, the busiest of the Inner City squares, is the Paris Arcade, with its quaint Moorish-Byzantine mood. The indoor shopping passage in the Arcade has a metropolitan atmosphere. Between the two palaces, there is a fine view of the Elizabeth Bridge and the waterfall below St. Gellért's monument, both illuminated at night.

The Vigadó of Pest. The architect was Frigyes Feszl, and it was built between 1859 and 1864 on the site of the old concert hall. Richly proportioned and symmetric, its facade overlooks the Dunakorzó and is an excellent example of the Hungarian Romantic style. Above the ground floor, orientally flavored arches, turreted columns and large semi-circular windows decorate the facade. The interior with the huge entrance hall, the stairway, the concert hall and the ballroom upstairs are lavishly ornamented. The frescoes on the main staircase were painted by Károly Lotz and

Vörösmarty tér. A rectangular square, it was shaped to be the continuation northwards of Váci utca. In the center, surrounded by a small garden, stands Mihály Vörösmarty's white Carrara marble statue with the Gerbeaud House in the background.

Váci utca. This is the pedestrian street no tourist visiting Budapest would ever miss. However, its character is of the present rather than the past. Even so, strollers may discover fine mosaics and wrought-iron work by looking up at the facade of the older houses.

Mór Than. Its opening in 1865 and a Ferenc Liszt premiere in the same year were the first in a series of many important musical events. World-renowned conductors, singers and musicians have continued to perform in the Vigadó, one of Budapest's largest concert halls.

St. Stephhen's Basilica. Budapest's largest church. Its centrally arranged interior is divided into nine parts. Construction began in 1848 to József Hild's neo-Classical plans. Its ground-plan is 85 by 55 m, the dome has a diameter of 22 m and a height of 96 m. After Hild's death, Miklós Ybl took over. His neo-Renaissance version fits delicately with his predecessor's work.

The exterior suggests its clear interior layout. The stepped main facade, with its arched vestibule and twin towers with a tympanum containing a group of Hungarian saints constitute a fine esplanade facing directly onto the Danube. Statues of the medieval Doctors of the Church are on the sides of the towers. Above the main entrance is a relief of St. Stephen, King of Hungary.

Unfortunately, sightlines onto the church are still restricted, even though much has been demolished in the meantime.

The Holy Crown. Pictures on enamel plates ornament the golden crown of the kings of Hungary. It consists of two parts: the upper, worked by 10th century goldsmiths, is made up of four cross-bands of darker gold, and the lower rim is of Byzantine origin and has eight rectangular enamel plates. The two were combined at the end of 13th century. The crown can be seen in the Hungarian National Museum.

Altar of our Lady, Patron of Hungary. This is the altar on the right of the Basilica. Gyula Benczúr's painting St. Stephen offering his crown and country to the Virgin Mary is flanked by the statues of St. Emeric and St. Margaret.

Inside the St. Stephen's Basilica. The main altar carries the white Carrara marble sculpture of St. Stephen (by Alajos Stróbl). The stuccoes of the dome above the altar were made by an Italian artist, while the bronze reliefs round the high altar show scenes from St. Stephen's life.

The Great Synagogue (VII., Dohány utca 2.). Europe's largest and still functioning synagogue, seating 3,000 worshippers, was built from 1854 to 1859. This was the first usage in the history of synagogues built in Hungary of two towers. The red and white striped brick of the exterior is decorated by ceramics. The style is a Byzantine-Moorish mixture, with a rosette above the arched main entrance and a main cornice with friezes. The inside hall consists of three naves. The interior yard with its arches on both sides invokes the intimate place of prayer of medieval Jewish temples.

Seven rooms contain the collection of historic and religious relics of Jews in Hungary, including antiquities, devotional articles and many valuable curios.

There is a Holocaust Memorial in the courtyard.

Szervita tér. The photograph is of a mosaic decorating the facade of an Inner City house built at the turn of the century. The glass mosaic on the roofline of the 1906 Art Nouveau building represents the "Glorification of Hungaria". Walking in the streets of the Inner City, there are many such surprises to delight in.

The Academy of Music (VI., Liszt Ferenc tér 8.). The picture shows Aladár Körösfői-Kriesch's Art Nouveau fresco entitled "And those who seek life make a pilgrimage to the source of art". The work is in the entrance hall of the Academy which provides the most perfect acoustics in Budapest.

The Opera House (VI., Andrássy út 22.). The Budapest Opera House designed by Miklós Ybl was opened in 1884. The state-of-the-art standards of the building is illustrated by the hydraulic stage machinery installed here for the first time in the world (as a measure of fire control). The imaginatively arranged interior spaces of the eclectic building present a marvelous view. The entrance hall is decorated by Bertalan Székely's allegoric paintings. The frescoes of the staircase ceiling are by Mór Than.

Represented here is the Royal Stairway, leading via the salon to the royal box from the left- hand side entrance.

The Vígszínház (Comedy Theater). Budapest's first private theater was opened in 1896. At the turn of the century, the theater-going public was captivated by the plays that were first performed here: at first mainly French comedies, then other plays from abroad and later still contemporary Hungarian plays. The domed Vígszínház has always been one of Budapest's most prestigious theaters.

The Auditorium of the Opera House. The ceiling of the huge auditorium resplendent in gold and scarlet, is dominated by Károly Lotz's fresco showing Olympus with its gods, the Muses and the Fates.
The three tiers of boxes are arranged in a horseshoe. In the center is the two decked royal box, behind it a salon featuring Mór Than's paintings.

The Hungarian Academy of Sciences. Opposite the large statues of a seated Count István Széchenyi and a seated Ferenc Deák, on the large oval Roosevelt square at the Pest head of the Chain Bridge, stands the Hungarian Academy of Sciences. It was built in 1862-1865 to Miklós Ybl's neo-Renaissance plans, then the fashionable style. Its noble silhouette is one of the landmarks of the Pest embankment.

The interior of the building has an eclectic atmosphere. The Academy has a valuable library, rich collections of manuscripts, periodicals and oriental records and craftsmanship. It also contains King Matthias' far-famed codices.

The Hungarian National Museum (VIII., Múzeum körút 14-16.). At the time when the other famous museums of Europe were being set up, Count Ferenc Széchenyi established the Hungarian National Museum. completed by 1846. The neo-Classical building was designed by Mihály Pollack. In the foreground is a statue of János Arany by Alajos Stróbl. Behind it, the simple but monumental facade with eight columns and a symbolic group of statues in the tympanum with the female figure representing Pannonia in the center.

The interior is less austere. A wide stairway branching off to both sides leads from the vestibule to the halls containing the permanent exhibitions.

The Market Hall (IX., Fővám tér 7.). Neo-Gothic facaded, this was designed by Samu Pecz and completed in 1896. There are majolica covered corner towers on both sides of the large pillared wall facing the square.

In the planning stage, attention was paid to the handling of the goods. A tunnel was bored from the bank to the basement of the Market Hall. The ceilings and the support structures are made of iron. The hall covers an area of 10,500 m² and it has become a favorite shopping place for visitors from abroad, too.

Western Railway Station (VI., Teréz körút 109-111.). This is where the first Hungarian railway station was built, from which the first train departed for Vác on July 15, 1846. Today's glass hall of 25,000 m² dates from 1877 and was built on the site of the original station to the plans and under the supervision of Gustave Eiffel's company. A significant part of the iron structure was cast in Paris. Crested, eclectic blocks straddle the gabled glass screen that faces onto the Boulevard.

THE CITY PARK

Here on an expanse of marshland about 2 km² in size, landscaping and the planting of trees was begun back in 1817. This, the largest of the capital's parks, had assumed its current appearance by the end of the 19th century. Ambitious plans were drawn up to celebrate the thousandth anniversary of the establishment of the Kingdom of Hungary and the festivities of 1896 were to take place in the City Park. Several temporary and permanent buildings were erected under these plans.

To make access to the Park easier, a 3.6 km underground line between the Inner City (Vörösmarty tér) and the City Park was opened on May 2, 1896. It was, in fact, the first underground railway on continental Europe. The convenience of this form of access promoted further development of the City Park.

Attractions such as the Zoo and Botanical Garden, the Amusement Park and the Grand Circus draw visitors in large numbers to the northern end of the Park. At the central entrance to the park stands the Millenary Monument, which is flanked on both sides by important art galleries; behind it is an artificial lake, which becomes a huge skating rink in winter. The bridge over the lake leads to the "historical" group of buildings (built for the Millenary celebrations) and the famous Széchenyi Medicinal Baths. The Transport Museum displays how transport developed; it was built in 1896, restored and enlarged following heavy damage suffered during World War II.

A whole network of shady paths interweave the Southern section of the Park. This part may also be considered an arboretum, because of its valuable collection of trees and fine mature plane trees along its paths. The beautiful garden is popular with all those who wish to relax and have some relief from the densely populated city.

Not least among the City Park's amenities is the Gundel Restaurant, which had and is now regaining European fame as a temple of Hungarian haute cuisine in an elegant setting. Apart from its private rooms and banquet halls, it also has a large garden, once a celebrated concert venue. The large central part of the City Park contains the historical group of buildings behind the lake; this was also the site for the Budapest International Fair from 1925 to 1972.

Theater performances are put on, using the King's Hill, in the City Park.

The Millenary Monument. Andrássy út leads from the Inner City to one of Budapest's finest open spaces, an enormous parade ground called Hősök tere (Heroes' Square). In its center stands an 85 m semicircular open colonnade divided into two parts. This too was built for the thousandth anniversary of Hungary's existence. At its center is a 36 m column with a

winged Archangel Gabriel on top, holding the Cross of Lorraine in one hand and the crown of Hungary in the other. At the pedestal, the equestrian group of the seven chiefs of the Hungarian tribes who conquered the country with Prince Árpád placed in the middle, is the work of György Zala

The semicircular colonnades contain the statues of 7 sovereigns on each side with bronze reliefs below them, showing scenes from their lives.

In front of the main column of the monument, a stone tablet was placed in 1956 with the inscription: "In commemoration of the heroes who sacrificed their lives for national freedom and independence." This is where wreaths are laid by foreign statesmen on official visits.

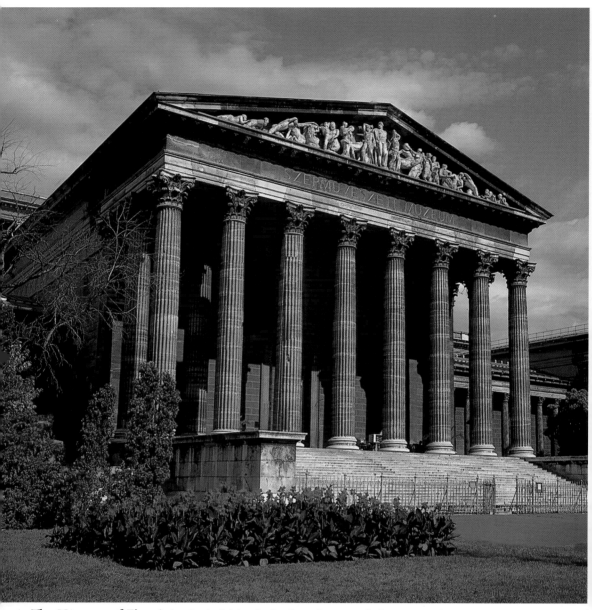

The Museum of Fine Arts. On the left-hand side of Hősök tere stands the Museum of Fine Arts, which opened in 1906 and was designed by Albert Schikedanz and Fülöp Herczog. The tympanum of this neo-Classical building contains a copy of a statuary group from the Parthenon of Athens.

The interior is Renaissance in spirit, consisting of halls of varying height, most of them skylit, surrounding the large, two-story covered central hall with galleries. The core of the collection in the Museum of Fine Arts was made up by Ferenc Széchenyi's donation, while the rest comes from public contributions. Some masterpieces have been transferred to other galleries in the city (including the Buda Castle). The current display contains a permanent show of Egyptian, Greek and Roman art, as well as well Italian, French and Flemish painting.

Temporary exhibitions are also held in the museum.

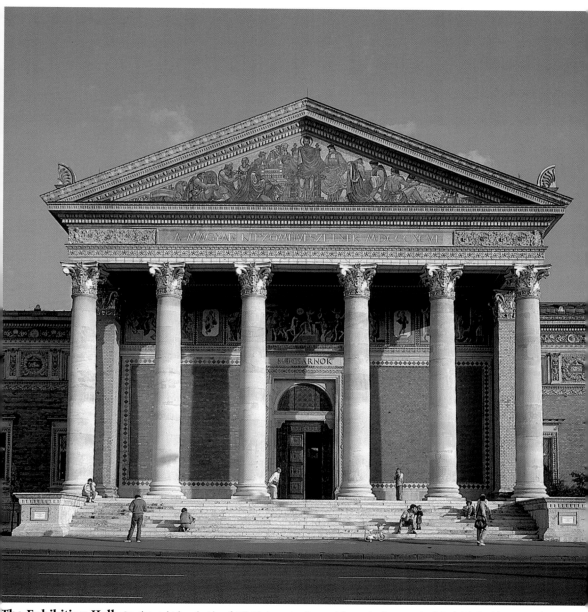

The Exhibition Hall. On the right-hand side of Hősök tere stands an elaborately decorated, plain brick building, Greek in flavor. This is the country's largest building devoted to the exhibition of fine art. Designed by Albert Schikedanz and Fülöp Herczog, it was built in 1905.

A wide stairway leads to the main entrance with six Corinthian columns. Paintings by Lajos Deák-Ébner adorn the building, al secco paintings by Károly Lotz are in the foyer which opens onto the skylit halls. The Exhibition Hall shows domestic and foreign work in every season. This is the largest venue in the capital for temporary exhibitions.

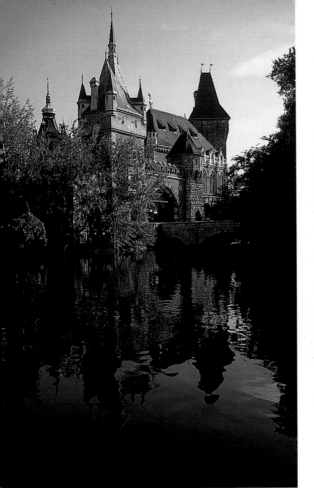

Historical group of Buildings. This make-believe castle was designed by Ignác Alpár, an erudite architect with a wide and inquiring mind, for the Millenary Celebration. The competition (1894) he entered called for a demonstration of all the styles that had been used in Hungarian architecture. It was first built in wood but was such a popular success that it was later constructed in the durable stone and bricks that are seen today.

The twenty-one part complex is divided into groups illustrating the Romanesque, Gothic, Renaissance and Baroque styles. The whole group, made up of authentic copies of historic

The statue of Anonymus. The sculpture probably commemorates the royal scribe of King Béla III, who surviving records indicate was the author of the Chronicle of the Conquest of Hungary by the Magyars. Presumably, he was in religious orders. Miklós Ligeti's statue represents him faceless, peering from inside a monk's cowl. Erected in 1903, the statue is that of the "nameless scribe", hence of Anonymous.

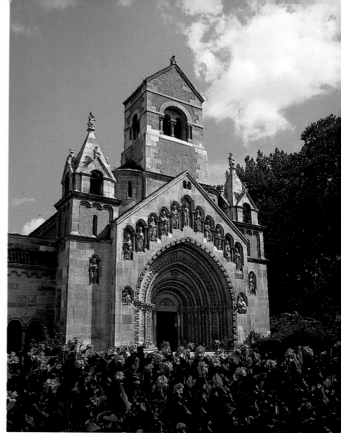

monuments in Hungary, has become a symbol of the City Park. Of its various parts, the best known is perhaps its imitation of Vajdahunyad Castle in Transylvania (photograph left).

One of the corner towers of its facade overlooking the lake recalls the Katalin Gate Tower in Brassó, the other represents the City Hall of Bártfa. Further parts show Baroque buildings in Hungary. Today, the building houses the Agricultural Museum and the Botanical Collection of the Museum of Natural Science. These invaluable collections are devoted to Hungarian hunting and shotguns, fishing and bee-keeping, animal husbandry and forestry.

At the Romanesque cloistered courtyard, there is an authentic copy of the main entrance, decorated by statues, of the abbey of Ják in Transdanubia.

The Zoological and Botanical Garden. It was in 1866 that the globetrotting scientist János Xantus was finally able to realize his dreams on a 40 acre plot that the city provided. Animals and plants from all over the world in and among the exotic buildings in an oriental style, pavilions, rocks and glass houses delight the visitor. The large lake is a paradise for water-fowl, and behind it is a bird-house. The Zoo's symbol is an Art Nouveau turreted entrance, flanked with large stone elephants on both sides.

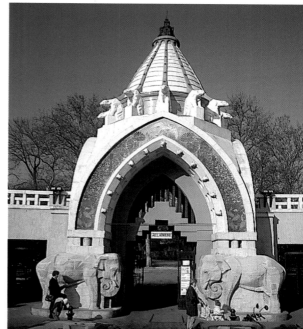

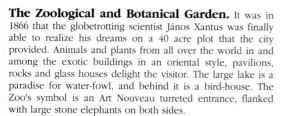

SPA CITY BUDAPEST

Apart from being a capital city, Budapest is also a health and recreation resort. No combination of that kind exists elsewhere. The reason is the subsiding dolomite layer underneath the city which spews thermal water from its cavities. The springs are on the surface in Buda and deeper - 1,000 m deep in the case of the City Park - on the Pest side. The fault of this dolomite layer runs along the riverbed of the Danube for a length of some 10 km here in the capital. The thermal springs along the fault yield 70 million liters of water at temperatures between 24 and 75 °C. The Celts who lived here in early history noticed this endowment. Later, when the Romans came they turned their settlement into a real spa, building a dozen baths. It has also been discovered that they also knew of the hot water spring on the small island north of the Margaret Island. Unfortunately, the remaining parts of this island were dredged away in the course of flood control operations. The Magyar settlers soon discovered the medicinal effect of the thermal water found here. Written documents dating from 1178 testify to the wide-spread use of the thermal waters here in the Middle Ages. The baths that developed under the Turks in the 16th century far outshone those known to the West, which lacked a tradition of the culture of balneology. The Pashas of Buda built nine major baths and remodeled those that had already existed. The baths of Pest have vanished without a trace and we only know of them from some surviving records.

Most medicinal baths contain pools of different temperatures, tub and steam baths and hot air chambers. The treatment of patients is supervised by specialists in balneotherapy from the hospitals attached to the baths. The thermal waters' healing effects are due to the fact that they may contain soil, calcium and magnesium, sulfur or radium. They are used for the treatment of locomotor disorders, rheumatism, indigestion, and gyneco-logical disorders. They are also excellent for drinking cures and for inspiratory exercise.

The waters from the medicinal springs now supply 12 thermal baths. Three large groups of springs are distinguished along the geological fault. Explorations have shown them to be interrelated: draining one bath was found to significantly deplete the water level in other baths, too.

Foreign travelers, diplomats and scientists have written countless records attesting to the amazing cult of medicinal spas found here.

Gellért Bubble Bath. The largest of the numerous medicinal baths exploiting the chain of thermal springs on the Buda side is the bath complex of the Gellért Hotel. Documents prove that these therapeutic springs have been known for time immemorial: this was the site

of the "muddy bath," or the building of the Achic Ilidgey, in Turkish times.

The Art Nouveau building, dominating its surroundings, contains a large pool with a series of halls about the basin, all of which are as decorative as the exterior. Medicinal water is supplied to the pool and the baths by 18 springs at a temperature of 48 °C.

The indoor bath illustrated in the photo was opened in 1934. It is used by local residents and the inmates of the 32-bed hotel-hospital in winter and summer alike.

The Wave and Thermal Baths of the Gellért Hotel. Open terraces and pools facing the hillside were built behind the Gellért Hotel. Most popular of them is the wave bath shown in the picture. It is open from spring to autumn. This calm swimming pool in the fresh air of the Buda side of the river, offers recreation to all. Waves in the medicinal water of the pool are mechanically generated at regular intervals, hence its name. The wave bath is primarily for amusement, while the richly decorated thermal baths inside the building are mainly used for therapy.

The Széchenyi Medicinal Bath. The medicinal bath shown here is found in the City Park. This early 20th century building exhibits features of the late eclectic style. Ornamented cones top the corners and higher ones rise in the middle. The domed hall is decorated by glass mosaics.

A well had been drilled on the spot as early as 1868. The first bath contained a common pool and tub baths. A new wing was added in 1926, which encircles large outdoor pools.

The water temperature of the spring supplying the bath is 76 °C. The medicinal bath operates throughout the year.

Király Bath. The history of the bath goes back to the Turkish rule of Buda. The typically Turkish building with its green dome was erected by the Pasha of Buda, Sokoli Mustapha, in 1566. It is Budapest's oldest bath today. The entrance section is more recent, being 18th century. The 41 °C medicinal water is piped into the baths, where the centuries are but as yesterday, and visitors can avail of a thermal pool, tubs and a sauna.

The Rudas Bath. It is not by chance that Sokoli Mustapha, the Pasha of Buda, had the most important Turkish bath complex built here. The 21 abundant hot springs of the Gellért Hill here yield 2 million liters every day. The domed hall, remaining from the time of the Turks, is supported by 8 columns, several stairs leading into the octagonal basin below. The thermal bath is only for men. The top of the dome is perforated by stained glass windows. Sunlight filters through like magic. There are smaller pools of different temperatures in each corner of

The Swimming Pool of the Rudas Bath. Stairs to the left behind the main entrance lead to the large indoor pool, whose size and beauty are illustrated by the picture. The medicinal thermal springs containing sulfur, lime and radioactive traces are also used in the swimming pool.

the rectangular room around the large pool. The bath, surviving since the Turkish occupation, was enlarged in 1896, with side wings designed by Miklós Ybl. The picture shows just this, as seen from across the river from the Pest bank.